# AFTMA'S POCKET GUIDE TO FISHING RIVERS & STREAMS

**Phoenix, Md.**

Distributed exclusively to the book trade by
Stackpole Books
5067 Ritter Rd., Mechanicsburg, PA 17055
1-800-732-3669

Special thanks to A.F.T.M.A. for their help in this edition. Also, thanks to fishing guide Mark Kovach, the people at Angler & Archer, of Rockville, Md., and Mark Susinno, a young artist endowed with the special talents to translate this information on to paper.

**Cover Painting by
Mark Susinno**

## ILLUSTRATION AND PHOTO CREDITS

Berkley, Inc.-12,13,19; Bill Burton-22,28,46,72; Cary de Russy-6; Eagle Electronics-87; Louis Frisno-24,25,26, 30, 31,32,33,34,35,36,37,38,39; Jim Guilford-4,54; Dean Lee-4,58; Dick Mermon-4; Rob Merz-27,42,43,44; O. Mustad & Son-8; PA Fish Comm.-27; Sampo-8; Somerville Studios-8,9; Budd Springer-5; Mark Susinno-Cover, 19,20,21,42,45,49,51,52,57, 60,61,62,63,64,65,66,67,68,69,70,71,74,75,76,78,79,80,81,82, 83,84; Zebco Corp: 16,17,18

Published by FIM Publishing, Inc.
P.O. Box 197, Phoenix, MD 21131

Printed in the United States of America

Pocket Guide to Fishing Series
**ISBN  0-917131-00-2**
Rivers & Streams
**ISBN  0-917131-02-9**

# To Our
# Young Readers

*If you're into drugs or alcohol, chances are this book won't do you much good. It's not that you won't learn something-you will. But, if your head isn't clear, you will miss the tranquility of a lake at sunrise, the serenity of a clear mountain stream, not to mention the delicate strike of a fish on the end of your line. It's really very simple, fishing provides its own natural high! No need for some mind altering drug. Besides, fishing under the influence of drugs or alcohol can be very dangerous.*

*Some people say that youngsters, or for that matter adults, take drugs to forget their problems. If you think this is the case, forget it! Your problems will still be there when you sober up, along with possibly a new one- drug dependency.*

*A lot of adults don't know how to fish. If you have never been, chances are the people raising you fall into this category. Why don't you suggest to them that you all learn together. Funny thing about fishing-with a little instruction, which this book will provide, anyone can be successful. You learn as you do it. You also get away from this hectic world we live in and get a chance to really relax. It's a great way to get to know someone, like the people who are trying to raise you.*

Marcel C. Malfregeot Jr.
Administrative Assistant
Harrison County Schools
Clarksburg, WV

# CONTENTS

# 1
# SELECTING TACKLE

Streams and rivers form the complex network of waterways that carry water from the highest elevations, eventually to the sea. Conditions of **temperature, water purity** and **flow** will change as the water moves through different areas and will determine the types of fishes you will find and the methods used to catch them.

One might logically think that the tackle employed to take on a swift river or stream should be bigger and heavier than that used on a quiet reservoir. But, such is not the case. The real secret to fishing these waterways is **to work** with the **current**, not against it.

Fly fishing for trout is the traditional method employed by a dedicated group of anglers, and is briefly covered in this edition. Since you are just beginning, and fly fishing requires a lot of advice from the tackle shop people or accomplished fly fishermen, we will confine our discussion to spinning gear.

A good all-around rod and reel combination is a reel designed to handle 4 to 8 pound test line and a matching rod with light-medium to medium action. This is called **BALANCED TACKLE**, and is at the heart of the selection process. It is important that your rod, reel and fishing line are designed to be used together. It is also imortant that your fishing lure or bait fishing rig be the proper weight for your equipment.

It is **always** advisable to seek expert help when selecting tackle. There is no such thing as a universal rod and reel, one that will do it all. Always buy your tackle from knowledgeable people; you won't regret it.

**Monofilament** fishing line is the most popular line in use today. It is made from nylon. All line is graded into **pound test** catagories. Ideally, 6 pound test line will break if you try to pick up a weight that weighs more than 6 pounds.

**Hooks** come in all shapes and sizes. For most river fishing in non-tidal rivers, you will be using the smaller series of hooks. This group starts with a #1 and is sized downward to #28.

**Sinkers** are lead weights used to get your hook to the desired depth and apply enough tension on your fishing line so you can feel the fish strike. There are many different kinds of sinkers.

**Bobbers** are devices used to suspend your bait at a desired depth. Always use the smallest bobber you can. When a fish

The drag setting on the push button reel is on top or near the handle. On the open-face reel, you will find it in front or in the rear.

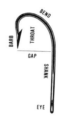

Anatomy of a fish hook.

**Plain Snap**  **Snap Swivel**

**Barrel Swivel**  **3-Way Swivel**

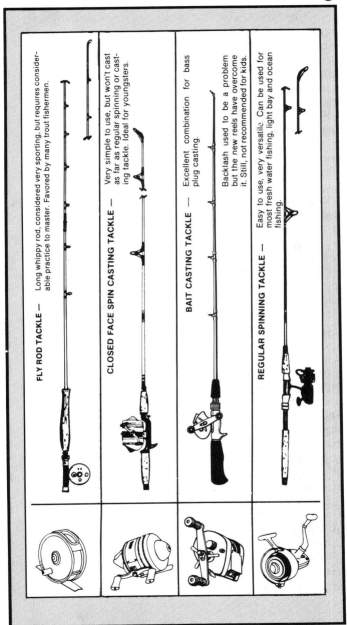

**FLY ROD TACKLE —** Long whippy rod, considered very sporting, but requires considerable practice to master. Favored by many trout fishermen.

**CLOSED FACE SPIN CASTING TACKLE —** Very simple to use, but won't cast as far as regular spinning or casting tackle. Ideal for youngsters.

**BAIT CASTING TACKLE —** Excellent combination for bass plug casting.

Backlash used to be a problem but the new reels have overcome it. Still, not recommended for kids.

**REGULAR SPINNING TACKLE —** Easy to use, very versatile. Can be used for most fresh water fishing, light bay and ocean fishing.

strikes, the bobber will submerge into the water indicating a strike. If the bobber is too big, the resistance caused may scare the fish away.

**Swivels** are devices used to prevent line twists. In river fishing, they will normally only be used when you are fishing with a bottom rig.

**Waders** or wading shoes are very important in river fishing. Chances are very good that a great deal of your river fishing will be done while wading. In many cases, tennis shoes will do. A good idea is to glue some outdoor carpet to the soles.

A **wading staff** is also a good idea. Commercial staffs are available at many tackle shops. If you have an old ski pole around the house, use that. You can also make your own staff. Find a sapling about 1½ inches in diameter and cut it off at about shoulder length.

As stated earlier, it is always a good idea to seek out advice. Your local tackle shop is in business for this purpose and it's a good idea **to follow** the advice they give you.

**Bass Casting Sinker: You may use this or any sinker that doesn't hold bottom.**

**Clinch on: Soft lead ears are clamped on line for casting.**

**Rubber Core Sinker: Preferred by many because it can be slipped on and off line easily.**

**Split Shot: Designed to be clinched on for casting.**

**Bobbers hold your bait at a desired depth.**

# SHOPPING LIST

| | | | |
|---|---|---|---|
| **BALANCED ROD, REEL AND FISHING LINE** | **LAKES & RIVERS** 5½' - 7' rod with 6 lb. to 14 lb. line<br><br>**SALT WATER** 6' - 7' rod with 14 lb. to 20 lb. line | **LINE CLIPPERS** | Always good to have for snipping off excess line. |
| **TACKLE BOX Big Enough for Additional Tackle** | **LAKES & RIVERS** **SALT WATER** Make sure it is worm proof. | **GOOD KNIFE** | Good for cutting live bait and filleting catch. |
| **BAIT BUCKET** | Useful in fresh & salt water. Keeps live bait, like minnows alive. | **BOBBERS 3 Different Sizes** | Normally used with bottom rigs. Match up with sinker sizes. |
| | | **BOTTOM RIGS (3)** | **LAKES & RIVERS** Usually called Crappie Rigs. Normally comes with hooks.<br><br>**SALT WATER** Usually called Top & Bottom Rigs. Should have wire leader. |
| **SWIVELS Packages of Each**<br><br>Snap Swivel     Plain Snap | **LAKES & RIVERS** Sizes #12 - #10 Plain Snap for lures; Snap Swivel for bottom rigs.<br><br>**SALT WATER** Sizes #7, #1, 1/0 snap swivels for bottom rigs. | **NEEDLE NOSE PLIERS** | Has many uses. Good for removing hooks and lures from fish's mouth. |
| | | **STRINGER OR BUCKET** | **LAKES & RIVERS** Either<br><br>**SALT WATER** Bucket |
| **SINKERS Assorted Packs** | **LAKES & RIVERS** Split Shot or Pinch On ¼ oz. - ¾ oz. Bank Sinker Kind ⅛ oz. - ¾ oz.<br><br>**SALT WATER** Split Shot or Pinch On ½ oz. - 1 oz. Bank & Pyramid 1 oz. - 4 oz. | **ARTIFICIAL LURES** | **LAKES & RIVERS** 1) Single Shaft Spinner 2) Plastic Worms. Sizes 6"-8" with 1/0-4/0 Worm Hooks and ⅛ - ⅝ Slip Sinkers. 3) (1 each) ¼-⅜ oz. Surface Lure. Medium Diver & Deep Diver.<br><br>**SALT WATER** Mainly used in trolling from boat. |
| **HOOKS Pack of Assorted Pack of Snelled** | **LAKES & RIVERS** Pack of plain hooks #8 - #2, 2/0 Pack of Snelled for bottom rig: Sizes #8 - #2, 2/0<br><br>**SALT WATER** Snelled, Sizes 1/0 - 5/0 with wire leader | | |

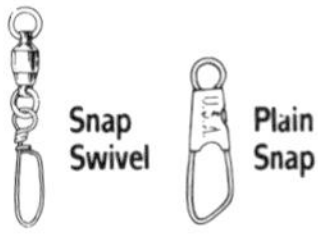

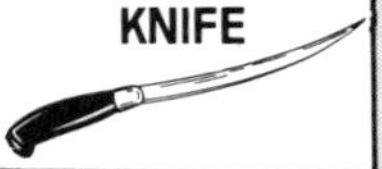

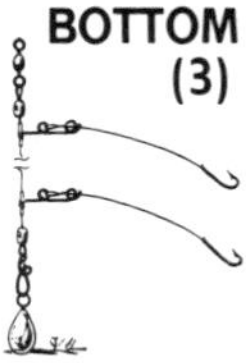

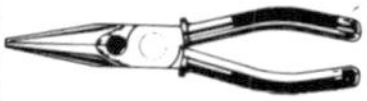

# 2
# KNOTS

**T**he knot is the weakest point in your fishing line and one of the main reasons for fish getting away. It makes sense that you should tie the strongest most reliable knot you can.

The knots demonstrated on this page and the next should cover most situations you might encounter. In the next chapter we will go into the proper casting techniques. It will be suggested to you that casting requires a lot of practice that should take place before you go fishing. It is also a good idea to become as familiar as you can with the knots that can make or break a fishing trip.

### Arbor Knot
The Arbor Knot provides the angler with a quick, easy connection for attaching line to the reel spool.

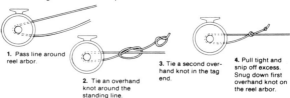

**1.** Pass line around reel arbor.

**2.** Tie an overhand knot around the standing line.

**3.** Tie a second overhand knot in the tag end.

**4.** Pull tight and snip off excess. Snug down first overhand knot on the reel arbor.

### Improved Blood Knot
The Improved Blood Knot is used for tying two pieces of monofilament together of relatively equal diameters.

**1.** Overlap the ends of your two strands that are to be joined and twist them together about 10 turns.

**2.** Separate one of the center twists and thrust the two ends through the space as illustrated.

**3.** Pull knot together and trim off the short ends.

### Trilene® Knot

The Trilene Knot is a strong, reliable connection that resists slippage and premature failures. It works best when used with Trilene premium monofilament fishing line.

The Trilene Knot is an all-purpose connection to be used in joining Trilene to swivels, snaps, hooks and artificial lures. The knot's unique design and ease of tying yield consistently strong, dependable connections while retaining 85-90% of the original line strength. The double wrap of mono through the eyelet provides a protective cushion for added safety.

**1.** Run end of line through eye of hook or lure and double back through the eye a second time.

**2.** Loop around standing part of line 5 or 6 times.

**3.** Thread tag end back between the eye and the coils as shown.

**4.** Pull up tight and trim tag end.

### Palomar Knot

The Palomar Knot is a general-purpose connection used in joining monofilament to swivels, snaps, hooks and artificial lures. The double wrap of mono through the eyelet provides a protective cushion for added safety.

**1.** Double the line and form a loop three to four inches long. Pass the end of the loop through hook's eye.

**2.** Holding standing line between thumb and finger, grasp loop with free hand and form a simple overhand knot.

**3.** Pass hook through loop and draw line while guiding loop over top of eyelet.

**4.** Pull tag end of line to tighten knot snugly and trim tag end to about ⅛".

### Double Surgeon's Loop

The Double Surgeon's Loop is a quick, easy way to tie a loop in the end of a leader. It is often used as part of a leader system because it is relatively strong.

**1.** Double the tag end of the line. Make a single overhand knot in the double line.

**2.** Hold the tag end and standing part of the line in your left hand and bring the loop around and insert through the overhand knot again.

**3.** Hold the loop in your right hand. Hold the tag end and standing line in your left hand. Moisten the knot (don't use saliva) and pull to tighten.

**4.** Trim off the tag end.

# 3
# HOW TO USE YOUR ROD & REEL

After reading the instructions for casting on the following pages, practice this skill until you feel comfortable with it. Now it is time for some target practice that matches conditions on the water.

Many fishing situations take place while you are sitting. This would be especially true in river fishing if you were in a boat or raft. You can modify the overhead cast to a side cast. However, this is not recommended because it is very easy to hook your fishing partner if you are not especially careful, which is always a good idea anyway. Restricting yourself to the overhead cast, place a target, such as a towel, about 40 feet away and practice casting to it, in both the standing and sitting position, until you hit it consistently.

Next, try moving closer to the target, and then about 10 feet further back. Again, practice until you hit the target consistently.

Your final exercise will involve casting into areas surrounded with cover. Find several trees with branches that hang down to within 6 to 8 feet from the ground. Place your target between the trees and practice casting to it, from a sitting and standing position, until you again hit it consistently. Again, move back about 10 feet and forward about the same.

## OVERHEAD CAST WITH
## CLOSED FACE SPINNING REEL

**1**

For the more accurate two-handed cast, hold your rod and reel as shown with reel handles pointing up and depress push button with thumb. With other hand, take line lightly between thumb and index finger.

With a slightly angled body, lift the rod until the tip is just above target (10 o'clock). Your elbow and upper arm should be close to your body, and your forearm parallel to angle of the rod.

10 o'clock

**2**

**3**

stop at 1 o'clock

stroke

drift

Lift your arms smoothly until hands are at eye level. Stop the rod at 1 o'clock and allow the momentum of your bait to flex the rod tip backwards.

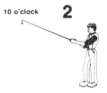

**4**

Without hesitation, stroke forward quickly and release push button at 11 o'clock to set your bait in flight.

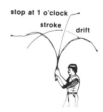

Follow through by lowering the rod tip to follow the flight of bait. If the bait goes straight up, you released to soon; if it flops in front of you, you released too late.

**5**

11 o'clock-release lure

**6**

As your bait nears the target, apply pressure to line with thumb and index finger of other hand for accuracy.

**7**

As you begin retrieve, let line flow through thumb and index finger of other hand.

## OVERHEAD CAST WITH OPEN FACE SPINNING REEL

**1**

Grip the rod and reel as shown. With free hand rotate reel's cowling until line roller is beneath extended index finger. Pick up line with that finger and flop open bail with other hand.

10 o'clock

**2**

Stand with body angled slightly toward target. Center the rod with tip top at eye level (10 o'clock). Position elbow close to your side; your forearm in line with the rod.

stop at 1 o'clock

stroke

drift

**3**

Begin by swiftly raising head almost to eye level, pivoting elbow.

### 4

When the rod reaches 1 o'clock, the weight of the bait will cause it to bend to rear. At this time bring rod forward in a crisp down-stroke.

11 o'clock-release lure

### 5

At about 11 o'clock, release the finger holding line. If bait goes straight up, you released too soon; if it plops in front of you, you released too late.

### 6

As your bait nears target, gently "feather" line with index finger. The moment it hits target, place index finger on edge of spool to stop flight of bait and prevent slack build-up on reel spool.

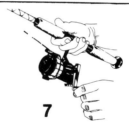

### 7

Without changing hands, begin retrieve. The line guide will automatically flop over.

**Pretend you are standing on 6 o'clock with your head under 12 o'clock. Your rod should be pointed at 10 o'clock. Bring it back to 1 o'clock, bring it forward and release at 11 o'clock.**

## OVERHEAD CAST WITH BAITCASTING REEL

**Reel may be held as shown or with reel handles pointed up, whichever is most comfortable for you.**

**1**

**2**

10' O'Clock

**3**

Stroke

Drift

Stop at 1 o'clock

Start Forward Cast

**4**

11 o'clock— release lure

Lower Rod tip to follow lure flight

**5**

Switch hands and begin retrieve

---

## SETTING THE DRAG & LANDING A FISH

An easy way to determine a good drag setting is to tighten it all the way then loosen it until it is just loose enough so the line doesn't break when you yank it off the reel.

"Pumping and reeling" a fish requires that the line always be tight. Raise your rod tip and as you drop it, reel in the line. Repeat the process until the fish is landed.

# FLYCASTING

Because the fly, on the end of your flyline, is practically weightless, you will be casting the line, rather than the fly itself. The basic cast with a flyrod consists of two equal elements: the BACKCAST and the FORWARD CAST. In both the back and forward casts, it is not the sweeping motion of the rod which

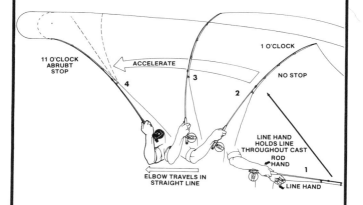

## BACKCAST

1. Point your rod at the water and remove all slack from your line with your line hand.

2. Smoothly lift your rod to 1 o'clock position, thereby setting entire flyline in motion. From this position, without stopping, begin to accelerate backward movement of your rod. Your forearm and wrist must be held straight, and your elbow should travel in a straight line. The backward motion of your arm is more PULL than SWEEP.

3. Maximum LOADING of your rod is nearly complete. Your arm and wrist should still be straight.

4. At 11 o'clock, stop backward PULL of arm and snap wrist back slightly, but quickly, to form a loop which will carry the line back.

throws the line, but rather the bow or **load** put on the rod by the sweeping motion and abrupt stop which allows the rod to UNLOAD, forming the loop which carries the line with it. **IMPORTANT:** No more power is applied to the forward cast than is applied to the back cast.

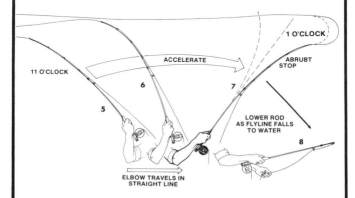

## FORWARD CAST

5. Just before your line has straightened behind you in the air, from 11 o'clock begin to PUSH forward, with your arm and wrist in the same position as in step 4.

6. Again, maximum loading of your rod is nearly acheived. Your forearm and wrist are still straight as in step 5.

7. At 1 o'clock, stop the forward push of your arm while snapping your wrist forward to unload your rod and once again form a loop.

From this position you can either allow some line to slip through the fingers of your line hand in order to add more line, and, just before the line straightens in front of you, begin another backcast;

or

8. After the stop has formed the forward loop, and as the line straightens in the air in front of you, you can allow the line to fall to the water by lowering your rod.

# 4

# FISH IDENTIFICATION

As you progress in fishing, it will become very clear to you that various species of fish react to their environment in different ways. It is important to learn these traits if you expect to be a successful angler. But, before you can master this learning process, it would be a good idea to be able to identify the various species and sub-species of fish by sight and that is the purpose of the chapter.

As you will learn later on in this chapter, freshwater fish are broken down into two distinct groups. Members of the trout family, for example, are **soft-rayed** fish. What this means is that their fins are soft and not spiny like members of the bass family.

Fish have brains, but not like yours or mine. Unlike humans, fish cannot reason. They do learn, but in a mechanical manner. Their behavior is governed by **instinct** and **reflex** rather than reasoning.

It would be impossible to list all the fish found in flowing waters in this chapter. On the following pages you will find illustrations of the more common game fish found in the streams and rivers of this country. Please pay special attention to the details highlighted on these drawings. In some cases, the major difference between two fish may only be the location of scales on their gill covers.

## RAINBOW TROUT

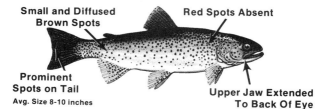

**Small and Diffused Brown Spots**

**Red Spots Absent**

**Prominent Spots on Tail**

Avg. Size 8-10 inches

**Upper Jaw Extended To Back Of Eye**

## BROOK TROUT

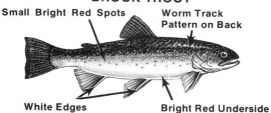

**Small Bright Red Spots**

**Worm Track Pattern on Back**

**White Edges**

**Bright Red Underside**

Avg. Size 8-10 inches

## BROWN TROUT

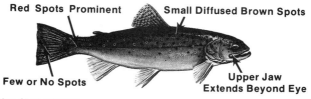

**Red Spots Prominent**

**Small Diffused Brown Spots**

**Few or No Spots**

**Upper Jaw Extends Beyond Eye**

Avg. Size 8-10 inches

## BLUEGILL

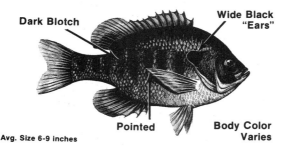

**Dark Blotch**

**Wide Black "Ears"**

**Pointed**

**Body Color Varies**

Avg. Size 6-9 inches

## CHANNEL CATFISH

**Greenish Gray Color**

Avg. Wgt. 1-3 lbs.

**Black Chin Barbels**

## LARGEMOUTH BASS

**Broad Streak**

**Spine Length Varies**

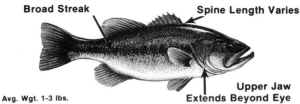

Avg. Wgt. 1-3 lbs.

**Upper Jaw Extends Beyond Eye**

## SMALLMOUTH BASS

**Vertical Bars on Side**

**Spines Closer to Same Size**

**Red Circle**

Avg. Wgt. 1-2 lbs.

**Upper Jaw Does Not Extend Beyond Eye**

## YELLOW PERCH

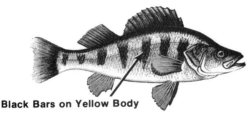

**Black Bars on Yellow Body**

Avg. Size 8 inches

## CARP

Avg. Wt. 5-8 lb.

## WALLEYE

Avg. Wt. 3 lb.

**Sharp pointed teeth on lower jaw**

**Milky Eye**

## NORTHERN PIKE

**Cheek Fully Scaled**

Avg. Wgt. 5 lb.

**Lower Half Gill Cover No Scales**

## MUSKELLUNGE

Avg. Wgt. 8 lb.

**No Scales on Lower Cheek and Gill Cover**

# EXTERIOR FEATURES

## SOFT-RAYED FISH

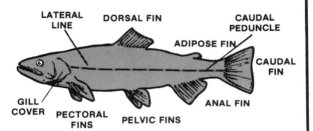

LATERAL LINE • DORSAL FIN • CAUDAL PEDUNCLE • ADIPOSE FIN • CAUDAL FIN • GILL COVER • PECTORAL FINS • PELVIC FINS • ANAL FIN

## SPINY-RAYED FISH

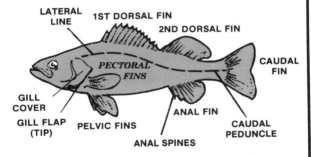

LATERAL LINE • 1ST DORSAL FIN • 2ND DORSAL FIN • PECTORAL FINS • CAUDAL FIN • GILL COVER • GILL FLAP (TIP) • PELVIC FINS • ANAL FIN • ANAL SPINES • CAUDAL PEDUNCLE

# INTERIOR FEATURES

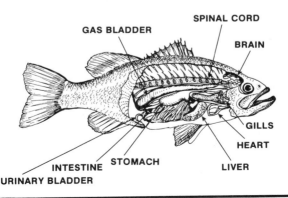

GAS BLADDER • SPINAL CORD • BRAIN • GILLS • HEART • LIVER • STOMACH • INTESTINE • URINARY BLADDER

# 5

# UNDERSTANDING YOUR QUARRY

Conditions on any flowing waterway are continually changing and this fact has a direct bearing on the location and availability of gamefish. A clear understanding of how various species react to their environment is of the utmost importance to the successful angler. In some cases, a realistic appraisal of the potential hazards of certain seasonal flows is an important safety consideration.

Topography, snow melt and rain levels will determine this fluctuation. In the spring of the year, melting snows combined with spring rains will create rushing water that carries all types of debris down these waterways and in some cases, actually changes sections of a river. As the season progresses, on most rivers, things calm down. White water rapids of only weeks before, become more tranquil, and portions of some streams and small rivers dry up leaving only pools of water.

All river systems eventually flow to the sea. At some point-in this journey a new element must be considered-tidal flow. This continually changing phenomenon is but another element that will determine the location and feeding habits of fish.

Understanding all these factors and how they affect food availability is the mark of a knowledgeable, successful fisherman.

## LARGEMOUTH BASS
### *Micropterus salmoides*

Found in every state, southern Canada and Mexico, the largemouth bass is the most popular game fish in this country. Although normally thought of as a large lake or reservoir fish, this member of the black bass family can be found in the slower stretches of freshwater rivers and many brackish (salt and fresh water mix) rivers.

Although this species can reach 20 lbs. in weight, the normal largemouth will weigh-in between 1 and 4 pounds. Generally speaking, the further south you go, the larger the fish, with Florida, Texas, Oklahoma, and Kentucky being but a few of the states that turn out large fish.

The largemouth bass is a cover fish. Logs, tree stumps, weedbeds and other aquatic growth are the kinds of habitat an angler should be on the lookout for when searching for this fish.

Known for its savage attacks of baits and lures, it is also thought that this species is the most intelligent available in freshwater. It has been noted that the largemouth will avoid a particular lure after only one encounter with it. Thus, lakes thought to be fished out, really aren't. The introduction of a new lure to these waters will often work.

There has been a great deal of transplanting and cross breeding with this species. The Florida bass, which reaches enormous size, is now found infused into the local strain in Texas and other states with a proper climate.

## SMALLMOUTH BASS
### *Micropterus dolomieui*

Unlike largemouth bass, smallmouth bass will normally be found in the cool, swifter sections of a river usually in the higher elevations. This species favors rocky bottoms though some will be found in weedbeds in the slower, deeper stretches.

Smallmouth start to feed in earnest when water temperatures reach the high fifties and are vulnerable to anglers just before they spawn, in the low sixties. After the spawn, the male will protect the nest and sometimes can be coaxed into striking a lure cast into that area. This is more to protect his young, than a desire to feed.

Also, unlike the largemouth, the smallmouth is rarely caught near the surface of the water, although sometimes during evening and early morning hours, surface bugs and flies will score. Being quiet is an important element in fishing for this species, as they spook a lot easier than their largemouth relatives.

Though normally thought of as a fish found mainly in northeastern waters, the smallmouth has been successfully transplanted to the west coast and elsewhere when conditions are adequate.

This species prefers nightcrawlers, leeches, small frogs. In the artificial catagory, try spinners, jigs with twister tails and deeper diving plugs.

## RAINBOW TROUT
### *Salmo gairdneri*

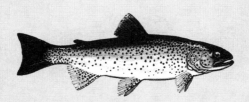

Considered by many as the most popular member of the trout family, the rainbow is the only true American trout. The steelhead trout is really only a rainbow that decided to spend some time, due to conditions, in the sea. Cutthrout, found in many western states, is a seperate species, but is also closely allied to the rainbow.

Found originally only in western streams, the rainbow is now available in much of the United States. The species spawns in the spring in waters with clean gravel bottoms and flow. Although their prime feeding takes place in waters between temperatures in the mid fifties and early sixties, they can stand water, for a brief time, in the eighties.

Most urban rainbow fishing is for fish raised in a hatchery. This group will go for worms, canned corn or cheese balls. Native rainbows will rise to a dry fly as well as the other fish getters in a fly fisherman's arsenal.

Like most members of the trout family, rainbows can turn off feeding for no apparant reason. It has been noted in certain areas, that the larger fish are only interested in live bait, spinners or spoons. Thus, the never ending mystery of the trout. As soon as you think you have them figured out, they change the ground rules.

# BROWN TROUT
### *Salmo trutta*

Brought to this country over 100 years ago, the brown trout adapts to warmer, less pristine conditions better than any other member of the trout family. A heavy, selective, insect consumer, the brown does its heaviest feeding right in the middle of insect hatches (55° to 62°F). However, when this species reaches a size of about 15", its diet will expand to include small fish, such as minnows.

While many a fly fisherman has given up with disgust trying to hook a brown during the day, for some reason everything turns around at night. Most dedicated brown trout fisherman ply their trade after dark with great success. It is common practice to locate a pool and stake it out, much the way a hunter would. The angler then casts downstream and slowly retrieves his offering over the pool making sure to leave a small wake.

Spring and fall are prime brown trout fishing seasons. However, it should be noted that the browns perform their annual spawning ritual during fall months and many states have a closed season for this species during this period of the year.

In many parts of the country the brown trout has been the savior of trout fishing. As mentioned earlier, they can withstand warmer, less clean water. Also, their suspicious nature insures that they won't be depleted from a water system.

## BROOK TROUT
### *Salvelinus fontinalis*

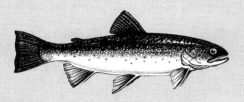

Earlier it was mentioned that the rainbow trout was the only native American trout. The brook trout is also native to these shores. But, it really isn't a trout. Rather the brookie, as they are commonly called, is a member of the char family.

Brook trout have very stringent likes and dislikes. Requiring temperatures in the 55° to 70°F. range, these fish also need very clean water to survive. Since these conditions are normally only found in high mountain streams that aren't very fertile, most brook trout never grow to more than 4" or 5" in length.

Brook trout aren't very particular in their dining habits if you can get close enough to catch them. Just about anything will spook them. Like brown trout, they are fall spawners and require spring fed waters with clean gravel bottoms.

In recent years, brookies have been transplanted all over this country. Normally found at upper elevations, they have done quite well. This is especially true in the western states where a population of freshwater shrimp are available for feeding purposes. In fact, in some western areas, the brook trout has become a problem because of over population. In some cases, state authorities have placed high creel limits on this species. This can be a bonanza to the trout fisherman who enjoys eating his catch.

# WALLEYE
## *Stizostedion vitreum*

Normally thought of as a northern fish, the walleye has been transplanted to many parts of the country and is even found today in the lower parts of Texas. Normally a nocturnal feeder, if you catch one, chances are there are more in the area.

Walleye are very rarely found in areas with a mud bottom. They prefer sand, gravel or rock. They are early spawners waiting only for temperatures to reach 45° to 50° F.

Not noted as great fighters in impoundments, this fish seems to be a more active fighter in flowing water. They are very careful in their eating habits and your offering has to be fished slow and at the right depth. A foot or two can make a real difference. Though not considered a worm feeder, nightcrawlers and minnows, fished on the bottom, are all effective.

Deep running lures, spinners and lures with a wobbling action will do the trick when fished with a slow retrieve at various bottom depths. If you catch one, remember at what depth you fished the lure. Chances are there are more available.

The walleye is actually a member of the perch family and can reach weights of 20 lbs. Look for them in the quieter stretches of rivers where they have been introduced, normally to help control the population of trash fish.

# PANFISH

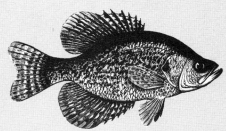

**Black Crappie**

**White Crappie**

Though normally associated with farm ponds and reservoirs, panfish will be found somewhere in any river system. Their numbers are many including the bluegill, crappie, pumpkinseed, redbreast sunfish, rock bass, white bass, yellow and white perch.

In general, these species are school fish, although their location within the many elements of a river system will vary. The bluegill prefers the slower currents of a river and becomes active once the water temperature reaches 65° F. They spawn between 65° to 70° F., and may be taken with live bait, small spinners, flies and spoons.

Crappie spawn at about the same time and are best fished for with small minnows or minnow imitations. As the year wears on and it becomes hotter, look for them near brush and downed trees.

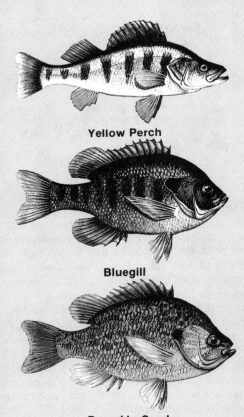

**Yellow Perch**

**Bluegill**

**Pumpkin Seed**

The redbreast sunfish likes a little more current and is especially vulnerable to surface lures and flies. Look for them on the outside bend of river curves after the spawn.

Though normally thought of as an impoundment fish, the white bass will move up rivers that connect with lakes. They hit baits hard and may be caught in great numbers when they congregate below dams and other obstructions.

The creel limit for most panfish is very generous if not non-existent.

## CHANNEL CATFISH
### *Ictalurus punctatus*

By far the most popular member of the catfish family, as far as anglers are concerned, the channel cat prefers clean, often swift waters. Armed with external barbules that it and other members of the catfish family use to taste, touch and smell, this species is fine table fare and grown commercially.

Channel cats are generally considered a live-bait fish, although spinners, spoons and deep running plugs have landed their share of this fish. But, in general, most anglers use strip baits, dough balls, corn kernels, worms and crayfish.

Other members of this family are not as particular in their choice of habitat. You can find them in areas that many game fish would not live in, such as the silted sections of larger, slower moving rivers. In fact, the entire Mississippi drainage is catfish country, not to mention most of the plains states and many parts of the deep south. Various members of the family have been introduced to the western states.

Though some will not agree, it is felt by many that catfish may be useful in feeding the world's population. Catfish turn food into flesh in a very efficient manner. Catfish farming is considered by many as a means of supplying important amounts of food in the future.

# CARP
### *Cyprinus carpio*

If there is one species of freshwater fish that has a right to have an inferiority complex, it's the carp. You either love them or you hate them. You think they're beautiful or ugly. More jokes have been made about how they taste than any other species.

They can get real big, not because they grow fast, but rather because they live for a long time- 25 years in some cases. You'll find them in reservoirs and slow moving rivers - the muddier, the better.

Carp belong to the minnow family and are related to the common goldfish. They are bottom dwellers who roil the waters by their constant rooting. In most cases in a lake, find carp and chances are there won't be any other species around.

Though normally thought of as vegetarians, this species can be taken on worms and minnows. However, favorite baits normally consist of corn kernels and dough balls. Carp anglers take great pride in their dough balls and the secret recipes they use.

High stream temperatures in slow moving waters don't seem to bother these fish. They can reach 10 pounds under these conditions and many grow even larger.

# 6

# LIVE BAIT

Live bait represents the food on which fish **naturally** feed. Unlike **artificial baits** that are designed to represent the **real** thing, live bait, when fished properly, appeals to the fish's sense of **taste**, **smell** and **vision**. Also, the movement of live bait can not be duplicated by its artificial counterpart.

It is especially important in river fishing to make sure you **match the hatch**. This term is a favorite of trout fishermen and usually refers to the emergence of various insects along a stream at different times of the year. However, it can also be used by any live bait fisherman when selecting the food his quarry is after. It is important to know what fish are **presently** feeding on when planning your trip. Fishing is a continual learning process. Never be afraid to ask questions. The bait dealer that services the stream or river you plan to fish should be a lot of help to you.

Live bait does have some disadvantages. For one thing, you have to catch or buy it, and it can only be used once. Since fish usually like their **groceries fresh**, time and money must be spent in keeping live bait alive. Also, fish tend to take live bait deeply into their mouths and hold on to it longer. This poses a problem because deeply hooked fish usually will not survive, even when released promptly.

# SHINERS

THE TOP HOOK      THE LIP HOOK

An excellent bass bait. The size of the shiner will determine the size of the hook used. With small ones use a 3/0 hook, with larger ones try a 5/0 hook.

If using a bobber, use the "top hook" technique. If casting a shiner, try the "lip hook" approach.

# MINNOWS

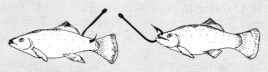

THE TOP HOOK      THE LIP HOOK

Great for bass, perch, northern pike and trout, to name a few. Minnows are smaller and more delicate than shiners. The "lip hook" technique for casting is the same as a shiner, however, the "top hook" technique for bobber fishing differs. Because this bait is so delicate, it is best to hook it behind the dorsal fin.

# CRAWFISH

Great for bass and panfish. Reserve large ones for bass and smaller ones for whatever panfish is in your area. Rig them as shown in the illustration.

You can buy crawfish at most tackle shops or catch them in a nearby stream. You will find them under rocks during the day and with a flashlight at night when they roam around.

---

# WORMS
## Earth Worms, Night Crawlers

THREADING
THE HOOK

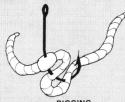

RIGGING
FOR LARGER FISH

By far the most popular live bait used by freshwater fishermen. There are several ways to correctly hook a worm. The more popular methods are illustrated above.

For small fish thread a section of the worm on your hook so they can't nibble away at your bait.

For larger fish use the method above, in the righthand illustration. For fish such as catfish and carp, fill the hook with several worms hooked using this method.

# GRASSHOPPERS AND CRICKETS

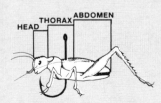

A lot of bait shops sell crickets and you can catch your own grasshoppers. They are very good baits and should be hooked through the thorax, as shown above. Make sure the hook barb is pointed forward.

When fishing a lake with these insects, add a split shot sinker to your line and fish it with a bobber.

# HOOK SELECTION

There is no fixed rule in hook selection and size. It's a good idea to use a heavier hook with heavy tackle and a lighter one with lighter tackle. Here is a general size chart to get you started.

| HOOK SIZE | SPECIES |
|---|---|
| #4 - 1/0 | Small bass |
| #3 - 4/0 | Larger bass |
| #8 - #6 | Smaller bluegill, perch & crappie |
| #4 - 1/0 | Larger bluegill, perch & crappie |
| #6 - #2 | Smaller catfish |
| 2/0 - 4/0 | Larger catfish |
| 2/0 - 6/0 | Muskie & northern pike |
| #6 - #2 | Walleye |
| #12 - #4 | Trout |

# 7
# FISHING RIGS

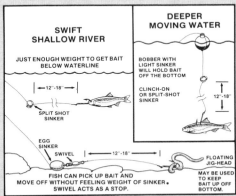

**SWIFT SHALLOW RIVER** - Add a split shot sinker to your line that is just heavy enough to get your bait below the waterline. If this does not produce, increase the size of the sinker, for added depth.

This type fishing is also ideal for using a jig. A jig is a round sinker with a hook attached. You may use live bait with it, or dress the hook with a rubber tail, feathers or any number of things.

**DEEPER MOVING WATER** - Add just enough weight to your bottom rig to keep the bobber up-right. Don't worry about your rig moving too fast, it can't.

You may also use the two rigs discussed above. The main difference is that you will have to supply the action to your bait that the current took care of further upstream.

For species such as carp, you will want to use a heavy, bottom holding sinker with your bottom rig. These fish don't like a moving bait.

# 8
# ARTIFICIAL BAITS

Although there are enough variations in the selection of artificial baits to fill a substantial textbook, this entire group of man-made fish getters basically fall into two catagories-those that represent actual forms of life and the other group that triggers reflex strikes. Sometimes, the only difference between the two catagories is color.

Forage selection in rivers and streams is usually determined by availability, and in turn, the availability of a given forage creature is usually determined by the season. Determining this pecking order is the key in artificial bait selection and sometimes it isn't as easy as you might think.

## FLIES

The traditional weapon of the fly fisherman in search of trout, flies are also used by some spinning tackle anglers and are divided into four general catagories: **streamers** and **bucktails, dry flies, wet flies** and **nymphs**.

Trout require cool water for their existence and are normally only found in upper elevations where these conditions exist, even though some states stock them in deep reservoirs, and urban streams. Many times their dining preference revolves around minnows and that is what **streamers and bucktails** are designed to imitate. These lures are especially effective during summer months when the hatches of stream insects are completed.

**Wet flies, dry flies** and **nymphs** are meant to imitate the aquatic insect life that trout will seek both on and below the water's surface.

# SALMON EGGS

Primarily used by spin fishermen in streams, **salmon eggs** represent the spawning eggs of **salmon** or **suckers**, and trout just love them. Special hooks are available at most tackle shops for these eggs and the addition of a split shot sinker is all you need add to your offering.

Even though salmon and suckers are only found in certain parts of the country, these baits are very effective anywhere trout are present. Fish them on the bottom.

# PLASTIC WORMS

A good **rule of thumb** for choosing the correct length worm to use is the faster the water, the shorter the worm. Thus, in the upper reaches of a river where the smallmouth bass is king, choose a worm of about 4″ in length. As you move down-river where the width of this flowing body increases, the water is deeper, warmer and slower in its movement, the length of your worm should increase to between 6″ to 7½″ to attract the attention of the nobility of these slower stretches-the largemouth bass.

In reservoirs and lakes, plastics are fished on the surface or below the water line with the aid of a special sinker and hook, as outlined on the opposite page. In river fishing these lures are fished almost exclusively **below** the water line, especially in the brackish section where fresh water meets salt water. As in reservoir angling, this bait is meant to be fished slowly.

DRY FLY - Adams

NYMPH - Gold-Ribbed Hare's Ear

STREAMER - Matuka

WET FLY - Blue Dun Wet

2

An example of one of the special hooks to be used with salmon eggs. All you need to add are the eggs and a split shot sinker.

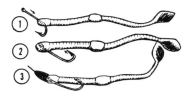

Rigging a worm "Texas Style". 1-Push the hook through the nose of the worm. 2-Pull the eye of the hook out just enough to expose it so that it can be tied to your line. 3-If you need extra weight, add the sinker before you tie your line to the hook. After your line is tied, turn the hook and push the point into the worm.

# SPINNERS

This family of artificial lures is normally broken down into two separate catagories and a recent addition makes it possible to add a third.

The oldest member of this group is the **single shaft model**. Graded by blade size, rather than weight, these lures are simple but effective. As with all artificials used in river fishing, the faster the water, the smaller the lure. In the upper portions of a river select blade sizes 00 to 1. Although single shaft spinners may be jigged, the normal way to fish these lures is with a steady retrieve. They are often fished with the addition of a live minnow.

The double bladed variety of **spinnerbait** is equipped with two shafts- one holding the blade and the other a molded jig head which is usually dressed with hair or a rubber skirt. This lure may be fished in a variety of ways allowing you to impart much of the action.

Unlike its single shafted counterpart, the spinnerbait is sized by weight. In the upper sections of a river have a selection to choose from ranging from 1/16 to 1/8 oz. In the lower stretches, increase the size to 1/4 to 5/8 oz. Although the single shaft spinners are not normally used in slow moving water, the spinnerbait is quite effective there and also in brackish water.

Recently a new member to the group was added. Closely resembling the spinnerbait, this new lure has a propeller instead of the traditional spinner blade. Designed to be retrieved rapidly across the surface of the water in lily pads and other aquatic grasses, the **buzz bait**, as it is called, gives off a sound similar to its name and is especially effective in late spring, summer and fall when bass are actively feed-

The single shaft spinner is a favorite of steam and river fisherman. Graded by blade size, it is most used in the upper, swifter flowing sections of a river.

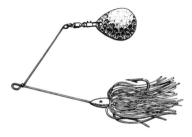

The double bladed spinner, or spinner-bait is sized by weight. This bait has proven successful for the entire stretch of a river.

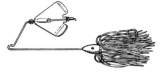

The newest addition to the spinner family is the buzz bait. Unlike its two counterparts, this bait was designed to be fished on the surface in a very rapid manner. The buzzing sound the spinning blades make is how it got its name.

**SURFACE CRANKBAIT**

**SHALLOW RUNNING CRANKBAIT**

**MEDIUM RUNNING CRANKBAIT**

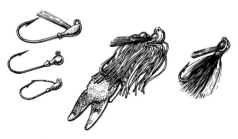

Jigs are very versatile lures. The 3 at the left illustrate what they look like without any dressing up. The top and bottom jig in that group are weedless, the middle one isn't. The middle jig is a weedless lure with a rubber skirt and a piece of pork rind. This lure is normally referred to as a Pig 'n Jig. The jig on the right is another weedless lure dressed with deer hair.

ing to fatten for winter. Fish these lures in slow moving and brackish stretches of the river.

# CRANKBAITS (PLUGS)

Rivers, by their very nature, are usually not as deep as reservoirs. For this reason, deep running plugs are not used. However, **surface, shallow running** and **medium running plugs** are used, often-very effectively. As with all artificials in river angling, the faster the water, the smaller the plug.

In the headwaters of a river, limit your size selection of surface and shallow running plugs to those 1″ to 1½″ long. Further downstream increases your choice to plugs in the 2″ to 5½″ range.

Most plugs fished below the water line have a built-in wobble. Some of the better ones are equipped with a ring attached to the eye of the bait. If the plugs you buy do not have this ring, tie your line to plain snap and attach the snap to the eye. If the lure does have a ring, attach your line to it.

# JIGS

Probably the most versatile of all artificial lures, the **jig** is simply a hook with a molded lead head. These lures are normally dressed with hair, a rubber skirt or plastic grub and many times can be made **weedless** much the same way the plastic worm is when rigged properly, or with the addition of a weed guard.

The name refers to the original way of fishing this lure-using an up and down motion of the rod. Often fished with the addition of live bait, such as minnows or worms, and ranging in sizes from 1/70 oz. to 4 and 6 ounces sizes used in salt water, these lures are a must in any tackle box.

# 9
# MOUNTAIN STREAMS

**F**ish are sometimes broken down into two distinct catagories; cold water and warm water species. But, as in all things, there are exceptions to the rule. The smallmouth bass is generally considered a warm water fish, yet it is not uncommon to find smallmouths and trout in the same water system. Trout, by their very nature, normally prefer cold waters and, in many cases, can not survive at warmer temperatures.

Besides temperature, the basic difference between a mountain stream and the head-waters of a river system is size. Trout are the gamefish most sensitive to pollution in any form and these waters are normally very clear.

Your state wildlife agency will provide you with a list of trout streams which are open to the public. These streams may be divided into two general catatories:

**CATCH AND RELEASE-** These areas are for anglers who enjoy fishing but aren't interested in keeping their catch. They are normally heavily stocked and provide good fishing most of the year. Tackle is limited to fly fishing and/or single hook artificial lures.

**PUT AND TAKE-** These are stocked streams that can be fished with any conventional tackle.

The holding areas for fish on these waters are smaller versions of larger rivers. Specific locations will be explained in Chapter 10.

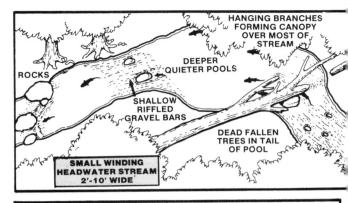

HANGING BRANCHES FORMING CANOPY OVER MOST OF STREAM

DEEPER QUIETER POOLS

ROCKS

SHALLOW RIFFLED GRAVEL BARS

DEAD FALLEN TREES IN TAIL OF POOL

**SMALL WINDING HEADWATER STREAM 2'-10' WIDE**

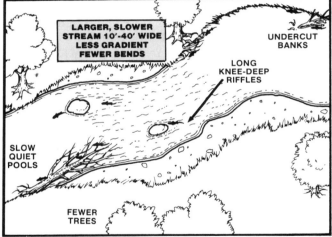

**LARGER, SLOWER STREAM 10'-40' WIDE LESS GRADIENT FEWER BENDS**

UNDERCUT BANKS

LONG KNEE-DEEP RIFFLES

SLOW QUIET POOLS

FEWER TREES

Trout streams in this country can range from 2' puddles of clear, cool water to 40' flowing water systems that are warmer and deeper. As the stream develops from its headwaters, to its eventual merging with a river system, the water system goes through many changes, both within the physicial characteristics of the stream and its adjoining shoreline.

The drawings above outline the development of a hypothetical stream as it progresses through its many stages. Notice how the trout station themselves in relation to the structural elements that are present.

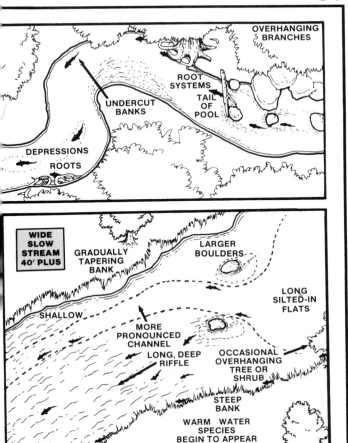

The most obvious difference between the headwaters and the wider, slower section that eventually merges into a river is the number of sharp bends present. With the elimination of these bends, the angler will find less undercut banks, great holding areas for fish, deeper riffles and eventually, a more pronounced channel. Also, vegetation will be set back further and the chance of fallen trees adding to the streams structure, lessened.

Eventually, species like smallmouth bass emerge within the flow.

# 10

# LOCATING FISH

In flowing water, fish are going to be where the **greatest** amount of food goes by and the **least** amount of effort is required to stay in place. Most spots in a river or stream with fast moving current lanes near slow water areas will hold fish. These fish take up residence in holding spots near flowing food lanes. They wait on the current's edge for food to be carried down to them. When they see something that looks appetizing, they grab for it-very much the way you would while walking down a cafeteria line.

Being able to identify these locations is **the key** to unlocking the door to successful river and stream fishing. A river's rocks, ledges, holes, bends and rubble all contribute to its structure. It may be above or below the water line, but has one thing in common - it causes the current to change speeds and creates pockets of slack water. Fish will inhabit areas that provide **food**, **comfort** and **protection**. Your targets for successful angling are these structures that create splits and pockets in the current.

Obviously, structure above the water line is the easiest to spot for the uninitiated. But, **sub-surface** structure can also hold many fish. The purpose of this chapter is to intorduce you to **both** elements of river and stream structure. It is important that you become as familiar as possible with these different elements.

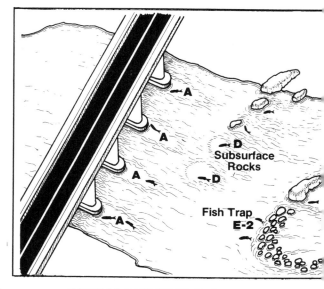

## STRUCTURE POCKETS

**A. SLACK WATER TONGUES** - Two currents are merging below the island, grass patch and bridge pier. Good holding spots for fish run along the downstream edges of the slack water created by these obstructions. Drifting your bait along the tongue's edges or criss-crossing the slack water can both be effective.

**B. EDGES OF CHUTES** - As water rushes through openings between ledges and rocks, current chutes are formed. Cast your bait to the upstream side of the chute and allow it to drift through the chute. Also, criss-cross the slack water behind the ledge or rocks.

**C. RIFFLED CURRENTS AND POCK-ETS** - These sub-surface conditions occur when fast flowing water runs around one obstruction after another. Interlacing through these currents are slack water pockets. Criss-

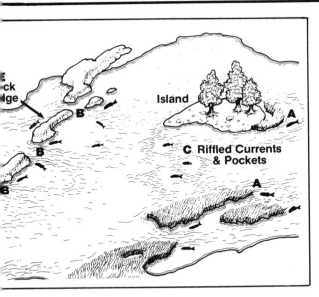

crossing the current splits is effective.

**D. CURRENT SLICKS & RIFFLES -** A large slick develops when water is flowing at a steady pace with no disturbance. Surface disturbance will appear when the water hits a submerged rock, log or other obstruction and pockets are created. Criss-cross these areas with your cast and retrieves.

**E. SLACK WATER IN FRONT OF STRUCTURE -** when flowing water hits a large surface, such as a ledge, it momentarily stops and then deflects off to the sides or over it. This type flow creates a slack water pocket in front of the object that will hold fish. An area like this is worth 3 or 4 casts parallel to the front of the ledge. Start about 15 feet in front of the ledge and work closer.

A sub-surface version of this structure is E-2. Here the structure is doing the same thing and your presentation should be the same.

# STRUCTURE POCKETS
### (Refer to Pages 60-61 for Overview)

## A. SLACK WATER TONGUES

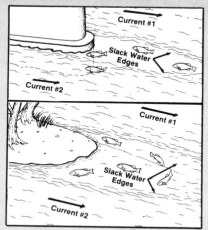

These tongues are formed when there is an obstruction such as a bridge pier, island or large boulder in the path of an oncoming current. The current divides into 2 separate currents to get around the obstacle and creates these tongues on the downstream side of the obstacle. Look for just about any species present in these ares.

## B. EDGES OF SHUTES

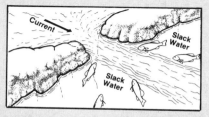

The boulders in this illustration cause the slack water. Fish, such as smallmouth bass, walleye and panfish will station themselves at the edge of the slack water looking for food.

## C. RIFFLED CURRENTS & POCKETS

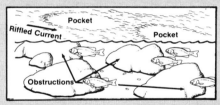

Riffled currents with slack water areas mean several underwater obstructions are present. Look for smallmouth, walleye and panfish there.

## D. CURRENT SLICKS & RIFLES

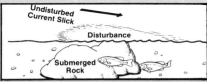

An undisturbed current that suddenly produces a riffled area means the water is hitting an underwater obstruction. Look for smallmouth and catfish.

## E. SLACK WATER IN FRONT OF STRUCTURE.

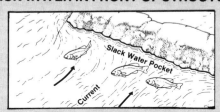

A pocket forms when water hits a large surface. Look for smallmouth, largemouth and panfish there.

### ARTIFICIAL BAITS

SMALLMOUTH BASS: Spring-jigs, grubs Summer-grubs surface & medium running lures; WALLEYE: jigs, grubs all year; PANFISH: small single shafted spinners, grubs all year; LARGEMOUTH BASS: Spring-Spinnerbaits, jigs Summer-spinnerbaits, buzz-baits, plastic worms, Fall-minnow & crayfish imitations; CATFISH: Spring-minnows, cut bait Summer & Fall-liver, minnows; CARP: doughballs, nightcrawlers all year.

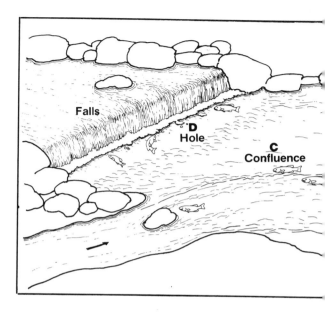

## SPLITS, CURRENTS & HOLES

**A. CURRENT SPLITS -** The bottom terrain in certain stretches of a river can cause currents to divide and merge for no apparent reason. In figure A, notice the fast water is creating little waves while the slack water is smooth. In this case, allow your bait to drift along this split or make several casts across the split in several areas.

**B & C. MERGING CURRENTS & CONFLUENCES -** Figures B & C show a quieter stretch of water. Here the currents are moving slower and merging into main food lanes. Fish will move to areas like this where the food is concentrated, the water is deeper and the current is not so strong. Many times these areas are identified by surface bubbles or

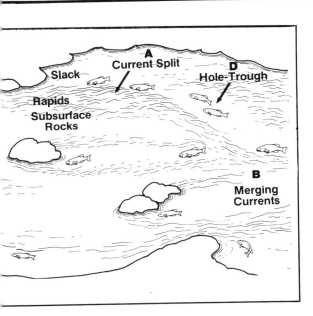

debris congregating on the surface along the lane.

**D. HOLES** - As the name implies, these are depressions in the river bottom. Fish enjoy being in holes for three good reasons: 1) food carried by the current settles out as it passes over them; 2) the current in the hole is slower than the faster moving water passing over them; 3) the depth of the hole provides protection.

The problem with holes is finding them. The surest way to find one is to walk into it. Since this is not practical, look for signs. If you come upon an area where the water is a darker color or the current slows, you might have found one. Fishing these holes requires that your bait gets down to the fish. Use heavier sinkers or allow your bait more time to sink before making your retrieve.

# SPLITS, CURRENTS & HOLES
(Refer to Pages 64-65 for Overview)

## A. CURRENT SPLITS

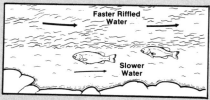

In this case, the bottom terrain is the reason for the riffled, fast water. Look for smallmouth bass and panfish in the slower, non-riffled waters that normally abut the shoreline.

## B. MERGING CURRENTS

Slower water normally means deeper water. When 2 slow moving currents merge, the result is a food lane for fish. You can normally spot these areas because of the bubbles formed or debris that is present. Look for smallmouth, panfish and catfish in these areas.

## C. CONFLUENCES

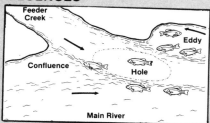

Similar to merging currents, the main difference being that here a feeder stream is merging into the main flow. Look for the same bubbles or debris.

## D. HOLES

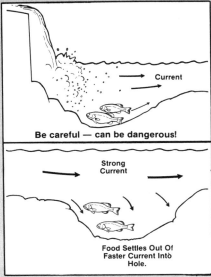

Be careful — can be dangerous!

Strong Current

Food Settles Out Of Faster Current Intò Hole.

Normally found at the base of a small dam or just about anywhere else in a river or stream's flow. Normally marked by darker water, these holes provide food, comfort from the stronger current above and protection from preditors. Be careful when fishing the base of small dams. The presence of a hole along with the turbulence of the rushing water can make these areas extremely dangerous. Also, make sure your bait is heavy enough to get down to waiting fish. Look for trout upstream and just about anything else as you move downstream, with the possible exception of carp.

### ARTIFICIAL BAITS

SMALLMOUTH BASS: Spring-jigs, grubs Summer-grubs, surface & medium running lures; WALLEYE: jigs, grubs all year; PANFISH: small single shafted spinners, grubs all year; LARGEMOUTH BASS: Spring-Spinnerbaits, jigs Summer-spinnerbaits, buzz-baits, plastic worms Fall -minnow & crayfish imitations; CATFISH: Spring-minnows, cut bait Summer &

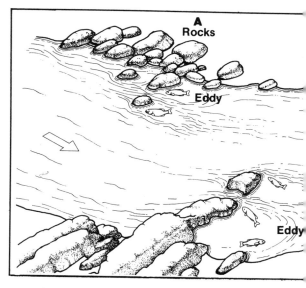

# SHORELINE STRUCTURE

As water flows along a shoreline, many types of habitat will be found. Usually shoreline water is shallow and slow moving, providing good holding spots. Deeper water nearby is ideal since this provides protection. Working the shoreline with consecutive casts as you move by may be the best approach, but there are certain types of structure that deserve more concentration.

**A. EDDIES** - Figure A shows an outcropping of rocks breaking the flow and producing a slack water pocket along with a reversing current known as an eddy. Casting into these pockets is something that should not be overlooked.

**B. FALLEN TREES AND OVERHANGING BRANCHES** - Other types of good structure, no matter where you are fishing.

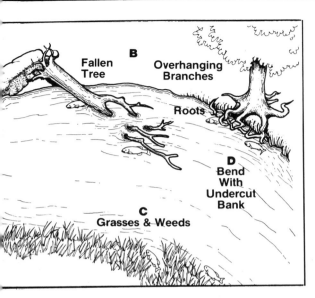

Figure B illustrates how fish may hold below, along, and behind a fallen tree. The tree breaks-up the current, shades the water, and provides protection.

**C. GRASSES AND WEEDS -** Grasses along a shoreline, as shown in Figure C, provide good habitat for insects and bait-fish. Fish will frequently cruise these grasses looking for food or hide in them while waiting to ambush a passer by. Presenting parallel casts along the edge of the grasses may just bring on an attack.

**D. BENDS -** A bend in a river provides another type of shoreline structure. Figure D shows how a bend deflects current back into the main flow. Food floating in the current washes up along the shore into waiting mouths. If the bend is extremely sharp, it may erode the shore causing an undercut bank which is known as the penthouse of river residences.

# SHORELINE STRUCTURE
### (Refer to Pages 68-69 for Overview)

## A. EDDIES

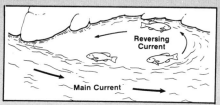

When an outcropping of rocks along the shoreline break the flow of a river, a slack water pocket is created along with a reversing current. These areas are home to just about any species except walleye, if they are present in your area.

## B. FALLEN TREES & OVERHANGING BRANCHES

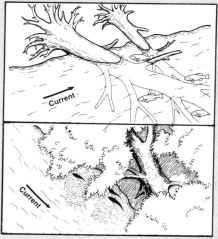

Fish, with the exception of walleye, if they are present, will station themselves behind a fallen tree in search of a meal that might drift by. It's also a good idea to try under overhanging branches where fish will, among other things, receive relief from the direct rays of the sun and some protection from preditors flying over.

## C. GRASSES AND WEEDS

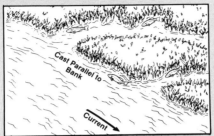

These areas are the habitat for insects and baitfish. Fish, such as smallmouth, panfish and largemouth will cruise these areas looking for a meal or hide in them to ambush their prey.

## D. BENDS

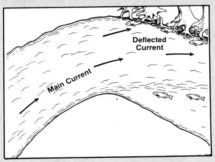

Look for anything but carp and walleye in these areas. The deflecting current will wash food to open mouthes. If the bend is severe enough, look for an undercut bank which should never be overlooked.

### ARTIFICIAL BAITS

**SMALLMOUTH BASS:** Spring-jigs, grubs Summer-grubs, surface & medium running lures; **WALLEYE:** jigs, grubs all year; **PANFISH:** small single shafted spinners, grubs all year; **LARGEMOUTH BASS:** Spring-Spinnerbaits, jigs, Summer-spinnerbaits, buzz-baits, plastic worms Fall-minnow & crayfish imitations; **CATFISH;** Spring-minnows, cut bait Summer & Fall-liver, minnows; **CARP:** doughballs, nightcrawlers all year.

# 11
# BRACKISH RIVERS

Anyone who has ever been to the seashore is familar with tidal changes. Every six hours the tides will reverse themselves, resulting in 2 high and low tides in a 24 hour period. There are a number of elements that go into the exact rise and fall during a tidal change. The most important element is the current positioning of the earth in relation to the sun and moon. Tidal changes in a geographic region do not happen all at once. Rather, it is a process that could have as much as a 4 hour **variation** between two points covered by the same **tide table**.

A tide table is a very important tool for any brackish river angler to possess. Produced by the National Oceanic and Atmospheric Administration, these tables predict the time each day the high and low tides will occur at reporting stations on both coasts and the Gulf of Mexico. They also indicate the tidal differences of different locations within the geographic region covered by a particular table. It is important to understand that tidal changes are the **most important** element in brackish water fishing.

Although the **fall** or **tide line** can often be clearly located, the division between fresh and salt water is a gradual one, often extending for many miles. These areas can be the home of both fresh and saltwater species but is normally considered the domain of the largemouth

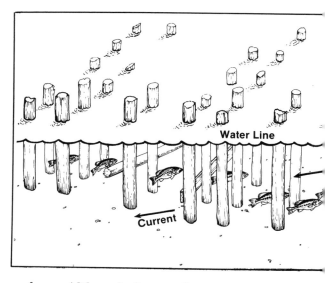

bass. Although the smallmouth bass is sometimes also present in these waters, the largemouth is better equipped to handle the salinity (salt) factor that these waters introduce.

From the end of winter through most of the spring you should concentrate your efforts on the larger creeks that feed into the tidal river. Although the surface weather may be cold, water temperatures can be perfect for bass and other species responsive to jigs with grub tails or 6 inch plastic worms.

At 45°F, bass become forage stimulated. When the water temperature reaches 55°F, the fish are greatly aroused and respond actively to lures. Once the creek water reaches 65°F, bass migrate to the main portion of the river in search of bedding sights to perform their annual spawning ritual. Don't give up completely on those creeks, however. Some bass will remain in these locations.

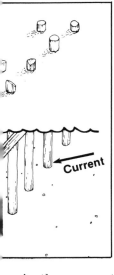

**Old piers and bulkheads are among the best areas to fish for tidewater bass as shown in the illustration on the left. The fish find food close to the structure, also utilize it to escape the force of the current. Fish as close as possible to areas such as this. Plastic worms and grubs are among the best baits.**

As the season turns from spring to summer, water temperatures rise and even though fresh water is still more dominant then salt, the warmer salt water now begins to have an effect on fishing. Lack of rain to replenish fresh feeder streams causes them to deteriorate and thus, the salinity level begins to rise. At this time a homogenization of the salty tides travels further upwards and once an area is saturated with an unpleasant degree of salt, bass move out and relocate. If, by some chance, this time of year enjoys a great deal of rainfall, this process can be delayed or in some cases, eliminated.

As autumn approaches, and water temperatures drop, bass return to the large creeks and along the river's shorelines, which is similar to that of lake migration.

The best fishing seasons on these rivers is spring and fall.

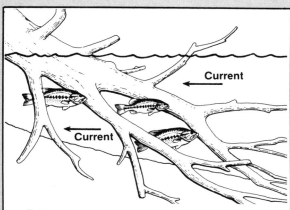

**Fallen trees and brush are ideal holding areas for tidewater bass. The trees provide cover, a place to ambush food and escape the force of the tide. Notice that the fish are facing the tide.**

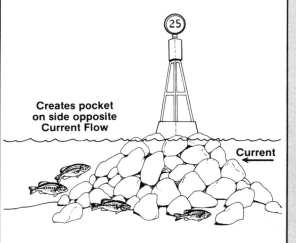

**Lights are excellent places to catch bass during tidal changes. The force of the current washes around such structure sweeping food with it.**

# 12

# PRESENTATION AND RETRIEVAL

**I**n chapter 10 we discussed the various holding areas for fish in streams and rivers. Obviously, these are the most important elements in fishing these waters, because **you can't catch'um if they ain't there**. However, presentation of your bait is also very important for several good reasons.

As stated earlier in this book, fish do not think as you and I do. Rather, they rely on **instinct** and **reflex** to survive. Granted, you can catch fish with poor presentation techniques, but the fisherman who has taken time to develop his skills will always be more successful.

**Never** be afraid to experiment in your presentation techniques. Just as no two people are exactly alike, no two fishermen fish exactly alike. The sport you are now reading about demands **creativity** and **trial and error**. As with life, the activity is a continual learning experience. That is what makes it worthwile.

As with anything, the more you plan your tactics, the better. When approaching a structural feature in a stream or river, stop for a minute before you cast and **survey** the situation. Plan how you will fish the area before you start.

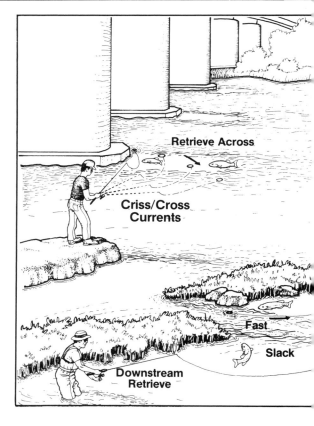

Retrieve Across

Criss/Cross Currents

Fast

Slack

Downstream Retrieve

## METHODS OF PRESENTATION

Once you've found a potential holding spot, how do you deliver your fly, lure or bait to insure success? Some variations of the following general presentations should work in most waters:

**DRIFT WITH OR WITHOUT ACTION -** Present your offering so it floats along the current's edge. Either a drag-free float may be used or one with twitches and pulsations to add some life.

**CRISS-CROSS CURRENTS -** Work your offering by throwing it into the slow current and moving to the fast current or by casting to the fast lane and running to the slow. A variation in retrieve speeds should be tried as well at different locations along the split.

**WORK UP AND DOWN CURRENTS -** Work your lure up and down the merge line of the currents, in either the fast or slow lanes. Stop your retrieve and allow the lure or bait to hold and work in the current. Also try twitching and jigging it.

# BASIC RETRIEVES

**Picture #1 outlines the basic retrieves of artificial baits in flowing water. Pictures #2 - #6 show how to fish certain artificials and list best situations to fish them as demonstrated in Picture #1.**

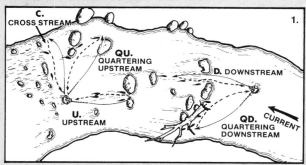

## SINGLE SHAFT SPINNER

RETRIEVES: ALL; BEST-QU

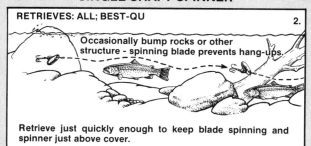

Occasionally bump rocks or other structure - spinning blade prevents hang-ups.

**Retrieve just quickly enough to keep blade spinning and spinner just above cover.**

## BUZZ BAIT

RETRIEVES: ALL

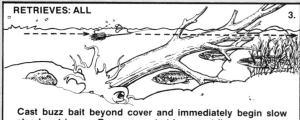

**Cast buzz bait beyond cover and immediately begin slow steady retrieve — Bump cover to trigger a strike.**

## PLUGS OR CRANKBAITS

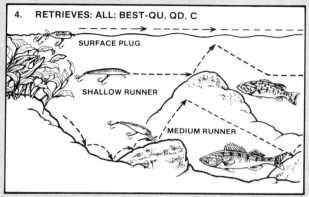

4. RETRIEVES: ALL; BEST-QU, QD, C

SURFACE PLUG

SHALLOW RUNNER

MEDIUM RUNNER

Occasionally pause retrieve, allowing floating/diving plugs to begin to rise to surface, then resume retrieve.

## SWIMMING RETRIEVE FOR PLASTIC GRUB

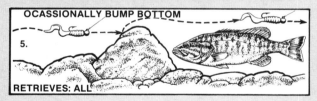

OCASSIONALLY BUMP BOTTOM

5.

RETRIEVES: ALL

## JIG

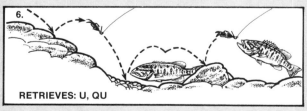

6.

RETRIEVES: U, QU

Pig & Jig — deer hair or rubber skirted, jig with pork rind. Keep slack out of line, watch line for 'twitch', signaling a strike. Work slowly. The same retrieve can be used for a PLASTIC WORM.

# PREVENTING DRAG

Fly fishing uses small flies that are almost weightless and thus, it is the line that is actually being cast. Fly lines are rated on the first 30 feet of line and are classified by a numbering system with the lighter lines being the smaller numbers. It is important that your rod and reel match the weight of the line.

Under normal conditions, small streams will require a light line (4-5) with wet or dry flies in the #12-22 range. For larger streams you will be moving up to a medium line (6-7) and selecting nymphs and dry and wet flies in the #8-16 range or #4 size bugs. In big rivers with heavy cover, you will need a heavy line (8-9) connected to #2-12 nymphs or possibly large wet flies.

ILLUSTRATION #1 outlines a major problem fly fishermen encounter. Since the fly represents a live insect floating down a stream or river, it is subject to the speed of the current. If this natural drift varies from the speed or direction of the current, the trout the angler is after will detect this and possibly be spooked, refuse the offering or not see it at all. This is called DRAG. Illustration #1 shows 2 types of drag. Illustrations #2, 3, and 4 show solutions to the problem of drag. These solutions may be used individually or in combination.

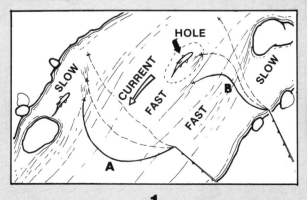

**1**
**A- DRAG CREATED WHEN CASTING TO**

**SLOW WATER FROM FAST WATER** - Illustration #1 shows a portion of the angler's fly line laying across faster water while the fly is traveling in slower water. This causes the line to belly (loop) down stream, dragging the fly across the water's surface and out of the strike zone.

**B- CASTING TO FAST WATER FROM SLOW WATER** - This example shows a portion of the angler's fly line laying across slower water while the fly is in faster water. Since the fly line is more resistant to the current then the leader and fly, the slower moving fly line will cause the fly to hang up in the faster current and swing out of the trout's strike zone.

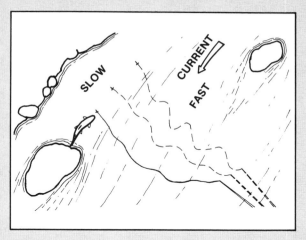

**2**

**SLACK LINE CASTING** is one method to prevent drag from ruining the drift of your fly. In this method, you put a series of S curves in your line before it hits the water, either by shocking the line when you stop your forward cast or by moving the rod tip from side to side after most or all of the line has straightened in front of you, before it settles on the water. In either case, you must allow more line than would be necessary with a straight cast.

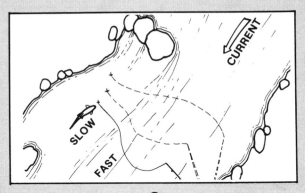

**3**

**REACH CASTING** is another method to insure a drag-free drift. In this method, lay most of the line upstream of the cast, when casting from fast to slow water or downstream of the cast when casting from slow to fast water. In either case, make sure your rod tip follows the path of the fly.

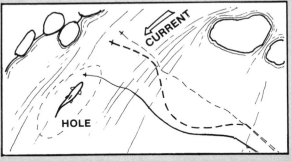

**4**

**LINE MENDING** is a third method of avoiding drag. In this method you mend your line after it is on the water by putting a curve in the line either upstream or downstream, as the situation demands, with rod held low and a flip of the wrist. To prevent pulling the fly when mending, it is often necessary to let out some slack line with your line hand as you execute the mend.

# 13

# ELECTRONIC FISHING AIDS

**W**orld War II introduced most people to electronics as we know them today. Sonar units became important tools in detecting German U-Boats and saved many a sailor's life. That same sonar technology is the basis for the depthfinders and recorders in use today. Many fishermen consider the electronics on their boat almost as important as their tackle box and for good reason.

Technology has been kind to this equipment. The advent of the transistor and other electronic advances allowed for the miniaturization of this equipment and today units are available to portray an accurate picture of a river's bottom and what fish may be present, measure the surface water temperature which is important all year long in determining the location of fish, and even indicate what color lure can best be seen in different water conditions and depths.

In tidal areas, **VHF telephones** may be used to call anyone in the world and in recent years, **Loran** units have become affordable for the average angler. Reading intersecting radio frequencies, these units are able to track on a nautical chart the exact location of an angler so that he may return to within 50′ of it on future trips. This can be particularly important in large water systems when your depthfinder or recorder has identified underwater structure that holds fish.

# DEPTHFINDERS AND CHART RECORDERS

After the knotted line and weight of Mark Twain's day, the first commercial electronic depthfinders were called **flashers**. These machines had a small light that rotated rapidly around a dial and indicated water depths. With practice, it was possible to determine bottom type and structure that was present in the area.

**A new version of the old flasher. This one has an alarm system.**

Technology didn't stop here. Soon **flasher-graphs** were available. Relying on the same technology as the flasher, these units printed out on paper what the flasher saw. They, however, weren't very accurate.

**An example of new video systems on the market.**

Next came the **straight line chart recorders**. Many feel these units are the best available. Most print out on paper, but video models are available.

**An example of an LCG unit.**

Recently, **LCG** units have hit the market. Displaying pictures on their screens using technology similar to a digital watch, one of the main advantages of these units is the ease of seeing the picture in bright sunlight.

**One of new LORAN units.**

With all these units, you get what you pay for.

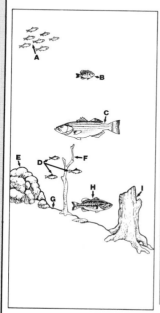 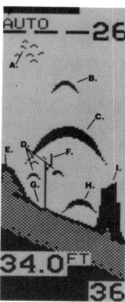

An artist's rendering of what an LCG is portraying on the right. The area shown is from 26' to 36'. The bottom slope runs from 32' to 34'. Thus, the total range covered is 26' to 36', with the bottom depth at 34'. Each dot represents ½" in height on the LCD screen.

A. School of Minnows
B. Small Fish
C. Large Fish
D. Minnows
E. Rocks
F. Small Tree
G. Bottom Slope
H. Medium Fish
I. Tree Stump

# 14
# SAFETY

There are few areas left in this country where the imprints of civilization have not left their mark. Fortunately, flowing waters in many instances, qualify as members of the select few. In many areas of the United States, pristine rivers flow through rugged forest areas as they did a thousand years ago, in picture book settings that are only forty or fifty miles from major urban areas.

Probably the last thing on the mind of most fishermen is safety. Yet, imagine wading one of these beautiful rivers or streams and having an accident. Who is going to help you? Unless another fisherman or camper happens to pass by, you could be in for real problems.

Good safety practices normally revolve around a little common sense. If you plan to fish a remote stream or river, it is always a good idea to let someone know exactly where you will be and when you plan on returning. This precaution makes it a lot easier for a search team to locate you if something happens and you don't return at the appointed time.

If you plan on fishing from a canoe or small boat, always check out the weather before you go. This is especially important in the Spring months when thunderstorms are a distinct possibility. Take it from someone who knows, the last place you want to be is in a canoe on a remote river in the middle of thunder and lightning.

Probably most accidents occur while anglers are wading. Your footing is at best tenuous on the slippery rocks and river bottom, not to mention the force of the current. One good rule of thumb to remember is, if you have second thoughts about your safety in wading a particular stretch of a river, don't do it.

Make sure you are properly outfitted with shoes or waders that are designed for the situation and a wading staff to help you keep your balance.

Even with the proper equipment, there are a few rules that should be followed to help ensure you are around for many more trips.

1. As mentioned, be **properly** equipped.
2. Always try to **stand sideways** to the oncoming current. By doing this, you provide a smaller target for the current to push over.
3. When crossing a swift area, **always** lead with the foot that is upstream, then bring the other foot beside it. Repeat the process.
4. If you are knocked over, **remain calm.** Keep your feet moving until you find the bottom, and your body upright until you are successful.
5. A broken rod is a **better alternative** than **drowning**. If you feel yourself falling, use your rod to stop the fall.
6. Hung up baits **aren't worth** your life. If your bait or lure gets hung up in very swift water, cut your line, because the few dollars you might pay in replacing it is a lot less then your family will have to pay when they bury you.

Wearing a hat or cap and a pair of gloves is a **good idea** in cold water. The hat will prevent the loss of body heat in cold weather and sunburn in hot weather. The gloves may appear to be incompatible with fishing, but some manufacturers are now making them very pliable, which allows for tying knots and accurate casts.

All river fishermen should have insect repellent and sunblock with them. The best repellents on the market are made from a substance called **DEET**. Be careful with this substance as it will damage plastics. The sunblock you use should be number 15 or higher.

Sun glasses are necessary outdoor gear, especially on a river when wading.

**Hypothermia** is the chilling of a person beyond that person's ability to rewarm the body. If not corrected, chilling of the body core temperature causes **weakness**, **hallucinations**, **uncontrollable limbs**, finally **unconsciousness** and **death**. Part of the body's protection is to sacrifice the blood flow and maintenance of body heat in the limbs to protect and maintain body heat for the internal organs and brain.

One fallacy is that hypothermia can only occur in cold weather. In fact, it can occur in almost any temperature, once the body begins to get cold or chilled through rain, wetting or wind.

This is a particularly dangerous situation for river fishermen. To prevent hypothermia, **dress warmly**. In the early spring months, it is a good idea to have several layers of cloths on. Make sure you keep your head covered and always have rain gear or a waterproof parka with you to help prevent against the **loss** of body heat.

It is important to remember that river fishing normally takes place in remote areas. If you come across someone who has succumbed to hypothermia, chances are you **will not** be able to secure professional help right away. In this case, remove their wet or cold clothing and replace it with warm clothing. If you have a hot, sweet drink with you, feed it to him. Under **no circumstance** should you ever give them alcoholic beverage. **Do not** warm the limbs and **do not** exercise the patient by walking. Warming the limbs will often cause **increased** blood flow to the limbs, resulting in **stroke**, **heart attack**, and **death**. In extreme cases, a warm bath with the limbs outside the bath is ideal. But, chances of finding a warm bath in the wilds is at best, remote. The next best thing is to **wrap** the body trunk in blankets or anything else you might have with you that will provide warmth. **Make sure** the arms and legs **are not** covered.

All river fishermen should wear a life vest. Known as PFD'S, or personal flotation devices, this safety gear is required if you are in a boat or raft, and in many cases, is more important if you are wading. There are 4 different classes of PFD'S. The first 3 are mean to be worn, and the fourth is designed to be grasped or thrown to a person overboard.

Types I and II will turn the wearer to a vertical position with the head turned backward to **prevent** drowning. Type III PFD'S are the type usually used by fishermen. They frequently have pockets and are often used as a vest. They will maintain a face-up position, but **will not** turn an unconscious person over. Many sizes are available in both vest and jacket styles.

Knowledge of basic first aid is also essential on any fishing trip. Normally you are in an area where medical care is unavailable and many times action should be taken before this help can be secured. The most common medical problem that anglers face is the removal of a fish hook that has penetrated the skin beyond the barb. Usually it's a good idea to leave the removal to a professional if you can get to a medical facility in an hour or two. **In no case** should you ever attempt to remove a hook from around the eyes, from the face, from the back of the hands or from any area where ligaments, tendons or blood vessels are visible.

The simplest removal is to cut free the rest of the fishing lure and use a loop of heavy twine (heavy fishing line is satisfactory) around the bend of the hook. Next, hold down the eye and shank of the hook, pressing it lightly into the skin. Grasp the loop and with a sharp jerk, pull the hook free. The downward pressure on the eye and shank of the hook clears the barb and allows it to travel out through the puncture wound. Be sure to have a **tetanus** shot as soon as possible unless such protection is already in effect.

Small cuts can be handled with antiseptic and bandages. Larger or deeper cuts require pressure directly on the wound to prevent excessive bleeding. To do this, use sterile, sealed gauze pads or as an alternative, an unfolded clean handkerchief. In the case of severe bleeding in which an artery or vein has been cut, a tourniquet may be necessary.

For cuts on arms and legs, the best direct pressure or tourniquet position is at the joint immediately above (closest to the body) the cut where the major blood vessels travel over or near the bone. Use direct pressure here, or a properly applied tourniquet, to stem the flow of blood. In either case do not apply too much pressure, or pressure for too long. As soon as it is possible, call a doctor, get the individual to a hospital or call paramedics.

# GLOSSARY

**ACTION**
Describes how a rod bends. Rods that have most of the bend in the tip end are called fast action while rods that bend evenly throughout their length are labeled parabolic.

**ADAPTATION**
The characteristic of a species to accommodate its basic nature to its environment to satisfy its basic needs of reproduction, comfort (security), and food.

**AERATOR**
An electric air pump used to maintain oxygen levels in live wells or bait containers.

**ALGAE**
Simple, photosynthetic plants with uncellular organs of reproduction.

**ANADROMOUS**
Any species of fish that lives in salt water and spawns in fresh water.

**ANTIREVERSE LEVER**
A lever or knob that prevents the reel handles from turning backwards as a fish tries to take line.

**BACKING**
A soft, strong fishing line, such as braided Dacron, that is wound onto a fly reel before the fly line is added.

**BACKLASH**
Line tangled on a casting reel as a result of a cast made when the spool continues to revolve after the line has stopped going off the reel.

**BAIL**
A wire half-round device that spools the line onto an open face spinning reel.

**BAIT-CASTING**
Name given to casting equipment that uses a bait-casting reel. The reel is also called a "level-wind" reel.

**BARBEL**
A whisker-like projection from the jaws of some fish, such as carp or catfish. They help the fish smell and feel.

**BLANK**
The basic shaft of fiberglass or graphite or other rod material on which a rod is built.

**CLASS LINE**
A fishing line which tests less than the nominal strength listed on the label. Used when a fish is to be entered into a certain IGFA record keeping category.

**CREEL LIMIT**
A term used by some fisheries agen-

| | |
|---|---|
| | cies to indicate the number of fish, by species, that can be legally caught in one day. |
| **DISSOLVED OXYGEN** | (DO): The oxygen utilized by fish which is put into water by forces such as wind, plants, micro-organisms, etc. |
| **DRAG SYSTEM** | A system of soft and hard washers in any reel that serve as a braking mechanism to slow a fish as it takes line off of a reel. Drag pressure is usually set to 1/4 to 1/3 of the line test. |
| **DRY FLY** | A fishing fly made of materials and a special dressing that allows it to float and imitate the adult stage of an aquatic insect such as a may fly or caddis fly. |
| **ECOLOGY** | The branch of biology dealing with the relations between organisms and their environment. |
| **ETHICAL** | Judging behavior right or wrong based on a set of values or options. |
| **FOOD CHAIN** | Chain of organisms existing in any natural community through which energy is transferred. Each link in the chain feeds on and obtains energy from the one preceding it and it in turn is eaten by and provides energy for the one following it as the food chains in a community make up the food cycle or food web. |
| **FRY** | Small juvenile fish that have just hatched out of the egg and up to several inches long at which point they become fingerlings). |
| **GILL** | An arch-like breathing organ located behind the gill cover on a fish's head. |
| **HABITAT** | The type of place where a species of fish lives. |
| **ICHTHYOLOGY** | The branch of zoology that deals with fish, their classification, structure, habits, and life history. |
| **KEEL FLY** | A fly tied on a special bend shank keel hook that allows tying so that the fly is tied with the hook point up, the wing tied to protect and make the point weedless. Designed for fishing in weedy areas. |
| **LATERAL LINE SYSTEM** | System of sense organs present in aquatic vertebrates (fish) in pores or canals arranged in a line down each side of the body and in complicated pattern of lines on the head. It detects |

| | |
|---|---|
| | pressure changes including vibrations (low frequency sounds) in water. |
| **LEADER** | Any material that is used between the main line and lure or hook. Can be lighter or heavier than the main fishing line. |
| **NYMPH** | A larval phase of an aquatic insect. Also, a fly tied to imitate such, used primarily when trout fishing. |
| **OLFACTORY NERVES** | Nerves that allow for the sense of smell. |
| **PHOTO-SYNTHESIS** | In green plants synthesis or organic compounds from water and carbon dioxide using energy absorbed by chlorophyll from sunlight. |
| **PREDATOR-PREY** | A fish that feeds on other fish. An interdependence between a species and an accessible and suitable forage. |
| **SCALE** | 1. A chitinous covering plate on a fish. 2. A method (scaling) of removing the scales from a fish for cooking and eating. 3. A gauge used to weigh fish. |
| **SEASON** | The period of time during a year that a particular species of fish may be harvested. |
| **SKIRTED SPOOL** | A type of spool found on open face spinning reels where a flange or extension from the rear of the spool to cover the cup and spool housing and prevent dirt and line from getting into the reel. |
| **SNELLED HOOK** | A hook that is pre-tied with a short length leader. |
| **STRUCTURE** | A term often used by anglers to designate any type of object or cover attractive to fish. Structure that fish relate too includes stumps, rock piles, log jams, piers, docks, boat houses, channel markers, points of land, etc. |
| **SUSPENDED FISH** | Fish which are hovering considerably above the bottom in open water. |
| **TAPERED** | A leader primarily used in fly fishing that is thick at the line attachment and tapers to a thinner end, or tippet, at the end where the fly is tied. |
| **ULTRA-LIGHT** | A name given to casting equipment that is reduced in size for casting small, lightweight lures. |
| **WEEDLESS** | A hook or lure that tends to pass through aquatic vegetation without picking any up. |

# QUESTIONS TO ASK

**M**any tackle shops in this country specialize in river fishing. They may be located on the river itself or many miles away in an urban area. It is important that you collect as much information as possible on the river you plan to fish in advance.

Make sure you have everything you will need before you go. Chances are you will be venturing into a remote area.

1. How high is the water? Is it too rough to boat down?
2. Are they expecting foul weather on the day you wish to fish? The first two questions are very important because you will be in rugged country and safety is very important.
3. Do the fish prefer live bait or artificial lures? What kind? Do you have them in stock? This is an important question because the answer will vary with the season of the year.
4. Do you have a map of the river?
5. What kind of structure is there in the stretch of the river I will be fishing?
6. In this stage of brackish water, where are the bass presently holding? What are they hitting on? Do you have a corrected tide table?

**REMEMBER, ALWAYS OBEY ALL SIZE MINIMUMS, THROW TRASH ONLY INTO A TRASH CAN OR BAG AND NEVER KEEP MORE FISH THAN YOU CAN USE.**